People Around the World

Life and Culture in
LATIN AMERICA

RACHAEL MORLOCK

PowerKiDS press™

Published in 2021 by The Rosen Publishing Group, Inc.
29 East 21st Street, New York, NY 10010

First Edition

Editor: Siyavush Saidian
Book Design: Seth Hughes

Photo Credits: Cover marchello74/Shutterstock.lcom; p. 5 Peter Hermes Furian/ Shutterstock.com; p. 7 AFP/Getty Images; p. 8 (top) Go Ga/500px Prime/Getty Images; p. 8 (bottom) Mario Tam/Getty Images News/Getty Images; p. 9 ullstein bild Dtl./Getty Images; p. 10 Culture Club/Hulton Archive/Getty Images; p. 11 Marios Savva/Moment/Getty Images; p. 14 AFP Contributor/Contributor/Getty Images; p. 15 Mario Tama/Getty Images News/Getty Images; p. 16 (top) Buda Mendes /Getty Images Sport/Getty Images; p. 16 (bottom) Anadolu Agency/Getty Images; p. 18 José Luis Quintana/LatinContent Editorial/ Getty Images; p. 21 (left) DEA/G. DAGLI ORTI/De Agostini/Getty Images; p. 21 (right) Craig Lovell/Corbis Entertainment/Getty Images; p. 23 MIGUEL SCHINCARIOL/AFP/Getty Images; p. 24 MARTIN BERNETTI/AFP/Getty Images; p. 25 (left) Topical Press Agency/Hulton Archive/Getty Images; p. 25 (right) Julian Finney/Getty Images News/Getty Images; p. 26 MARTIN BERNETTI/AFP/Getty Images; p. 28 Werner Forman/Universal Images Group/Getty Images; p. 29 DEA/G. DAGLI ORTI/De Agostini/Getty Images; p. 30 (top) Matej Divizna/ Getty Images Entertainment/Getty Images; p. 30 (bottom) Santi Visalli/Archive Photos/Getty Images; p. 34 Jeff Greenberg/Universal Images Group/Getty Images; p. 36 (left) DANIEL LEAL-OLIVAS/AFP/Getty Images; p. 36 (right) Hulton Archive/Archive Photos/Getty Images; p. 37 (left) ampueroleonardo/E+/Getty Images; p. 37 (right) Dan Kitwood/Getty Images News/Getty Images; p. 38 Zeroth/Wikimedia Commons; p. 41 Art Rickerby/The LIFE Picture Collection/Getty Images; p. 42 Getty Images/Hulton Archive/Getty Images; p. 43 (top) Kevin Winter/Getty Images Entertainment/Getty Images; p. 43 (bottom) Frazer Harrison/Getty Images Entertainment/Getty Images; p. 44 Mario Tama/Getty Images News/Getty Images; p. 45 Chicago Tribune/Contributor/Tribune News Service/Getty Images.

Cataloging-in-Publication Data

Names: Morlock, Rachael.
Title: Life and culture in Latin America / Rachael Morlock.
Description: New York : PowerKids Press, 2021. | Series: People around the world
  | Includes glossary and index.
Identifiers: ISBN 9781725321564 (pbk.) | ISBN 9781725321588 (library bound)
  | ISBN 9781725321571 (6 pack) | ISBN 9781725321595 (ebook)
Subjects: LCSH: Latin America–Juvenile literature. | Latin America–Social life and customs–Juvenile literature. | Latin America–Intellectual life–Juvenile literature. | Latin America–Social conditions–Juvenile literature.
Classification: LCC F1408.3 M667 2020 | DDC 980–dc23

Manufactured in the United States of America

Find us on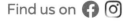

Contents

Introduction
A LOOK AT LATIN AMERICA

Colorful festivals, bold art, catchy rhythms, innovative literature, and a rich ancient and modern history—all of these are part of Latin American culture. Latin America isn't a continent or country. Rather, it's a sprawling region with **diverse** peoples and cultures. It includes 24 nations and 5 territories in North America, the Caribbean, and South America. It stretches from Mexico in the north to the tip of Chile in the south. More than 641 million people live in this region, which covers about 13 percent of Earth's total land surface area.

The word "Latin" refers to the languages spoken in the region. It also speaks to the influence and history of colonization in the area. European settlers imported Latin-based languages to the area beginning in the late 1400s. As a result, Spanish and Portuguese are the dominant languages in the region today.

Each country and ethnic group in Latin America has its own distinct identity. However, the people throughout this region also share many aspects of their history and culture. Ideas, beliefs, and practices have spread across the region for thousands of years. Important cultural contributions by Latin American individuals and communities have long been recognized and valued around the world.

UNITED STATES

MEXICO

CUBA

DOMINICAN REPUBLIC

HAITI

BELIZE

GUATEMALA HONDURAS

EL SALVADOR

NICARAGUA

COSTA RICA

PANAMA

VENEZUELA

GUYANA

SURINAME

French Guiana (FRANCE)

COLOMBIA

ECUADOR

B R A Z I L

PERU

BOLIVIA

PARAGUAY

You won't necessarily see the name "Latin America" on a map. The term refers to a large region that includes countries and territories south of the United States where Spanish, Portuguese, and French are spoken.

CHILE

URUGUAY

ARGENTINA

1 DIVERSE DEMOGRAPHICS

The rich diversity of Latin America is the result of a long and **multicultural** history. Scientific evidence suggests that humans traveled down the Pacific coast of North America and into Central and South America more than 14,000 years ago. Over the centuries, small **nomadic** groups in the region developed into organized civilizations. The three most advanced societies to emerge from Latin America were the Maya in Mesoamerica, the Aztec people in Mexico, and the Inca in Peru. Their achievements remain important sources of pride and wonder in modern Latin American culture.

A new era began when Christopher Columbus landed on the island of Hispaniola in 1492. He was the first in a wave of explorers

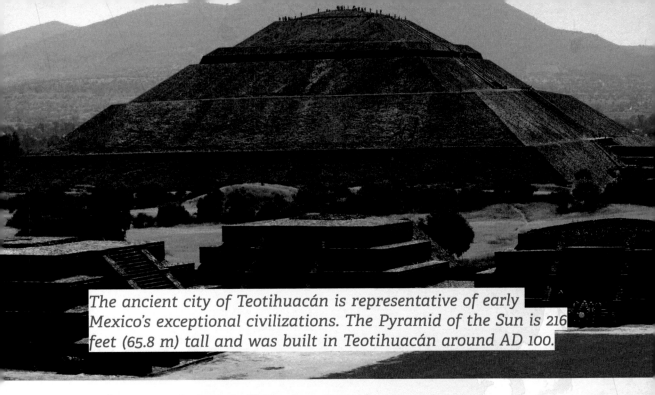

The ancient city of Teotihuacán is representative of early Mexico's exceptional civilizations. The Pyramid of the Sun is 216 feet (65.8 m) tall and was built in Teotihuacán around AD 100.

who participated in a period of conquest, **colonization**, and major change in the Americas. Spain, Portugal, and other European powers laid claim to Latin American land and resources. Europeans swept across the region with imported guns and diseases, severely damaging native populations and establishing new settlements.

CULTURAL CONNECTIONS

The first people Christopher Columbus met in Hispaniola were the Taino. Conquered by the Spanish in 1493, the Taino were nearly extinct by 1560 as a result of disease, violence, and slavery.

The Spanish conquered the Inca Empire in 1535, but its legacy and achievements live on. Machu Picchu, an ancient Incan city, is a powerful cultural symbol in Peru.

Afro-descendants hold a celebration in Rio de Janeiro, Brazil, the point of entry for nearly a million Africans. Overall, 4 million Africans were enslaved in Brazil.

Latin American populations changed dramatically as settlers arrived from Europe. **Indigenous** peoples were enslaved, pushed out of urban centers, or integrated into European settlements as the lowest rung in the social **hierarchy**. The transatlantic slave trade introduced a new element to the **Columbian Exchange**. From the 16th century through the 19th century, millions of Africans were ripped from their homeland and transported to the Americas. Many were forced to labor in mines, sugar plantations, and tobacco fields in Brazil and the Caribbean.

Women in Latin America

Gender equality is a problem throughout Latin America. One way this manifests is in a significant pay gap: on average, women earn 16 percent less than men. However, women attend secondary school about as much as men. Though there is room for improvement, Latin American countries have paved the way toward equality by electing female heads of state. Women have served as president in Nicaragua, Panama, Chile, Argentina, Costa Rica, and Brazil. In addition, eight Latin American countries require that half their lawmakers are women, and others reserve spaces for female public servants. As women are better represented in government, other gender inequalities are likely to decrease.

In 1990, Violeta Chamorro of Nicaragua became the first woman in the Western Hemisphere to be elected president of a country.

Columbian Exchange: An interchange of plants, animals, disease, people, and culture between the Western and Eastern Hemispheres following the voyages of Columbus.

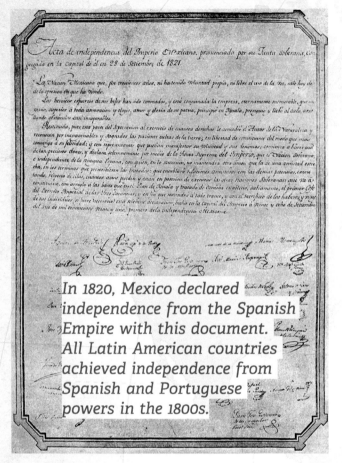

In 1820, Mexico declared independence from the Spanish Empire with this document. All Latin American countries achieved independence from Spanish and Portuguese powers in the 1800s.

Over three centuries of colonial rule, the main Latin American ethnic groups—people of indigenous, European, or African descent—became increasingly mixed. A strict social class structure was put in place. More power was given to people born in Europe or people of European descent. People of mixed European

CULTURAL CONNECTIONS

Latin America has also seen many **immigrants** from around the world, including the Middle East, Europe, and Asia. In fact, Brazil has the largest Japanese population outside of Japan.

and indigenous heritage had less power, while people of African descent or of purely indigenous descent had even less. The colonial class structure doesn't exist in the same way today, but ethnic groups have continued to mix and diversify the population.

In terms of **demography**, Latin America's multiculturalism is still evident today. Indigenous groups with pre-Columbian ties are predominantly found in Mexico, Peru, Guatemala, Bolivia,

At the Otavalo Market in Ecuador, locals sell traditional handcrafts and regional foods. Ecuador has one of the largest indigenous populations in Latin America.

Urban Life

Latin America was home to about 8 percent of the world's population in 2019, and more than 80 percent of Latin Americans live in urban centers. Mexico City, Mexico, and São Paulo, Brazil, are the two most populous cities in Latin America with more than 21 million residents each. Buenos Aires in Argentina, Rio de Janeiro in Brazil, Lima in Peru, and Bogotá in Colombia are also major cities. However, social inequality—paired with rapid urban growth—has led to many problems. Poverty is a struggle throughout the region, and bustling cities fall short in providing housing, clean water, and safe living conditions for some of their poorer residents.

and Ecuador. Large populations of Latin Americans with a blend of European and indigenous roots live in Colombia, Mexico, Nicaragua, Panama, and Venezuela. Afro-descendant Latin Americans make up substantial portions of the population in Brazil, Cuba, the Dominican Republic, Puerto Rico, and Haiti.

2 RELIGIONS AND FESTIVALS

L ike much of Latin American culture, the area's religions have been shaped by indigenous, European, and African forces. Religious beliefs and practices from pre-Columbian cultures were passed down through the generations. They remain strongest in remote areas, where the influence of European settlers was less intense. In places with greater **cultural diffusion** and exchange, indigenous religions blended with European traditions.

CULTURAL CONNECTIONS

Shamanism and **animism** are practiced in Latin America, mostly in isolated indigenous communities in the Amazon or Andes. These religions pursue connections with natural spirits and forces.

animism: A belief that objects, places, and creatures have living spirits.

cultural diffusion: The process of spreading cultural traits from one

Inti Raymi is a winter **solstice** festival tied to traditional Incan beliefs in the Peruvian Andes. A colorful ceremony is part of the celebration near Cuzco, Peru.

Christianity spread quickly across Latin America during the colonial era. Spain and Portugal were Catholic countries, and Roman Catholicism was one of their main imports to new colonies. Indigenous religious practices were often outlawed, and native populations were forced to convert to Catholicism.

CULTURAL CONNECTIONS

In Mexico, Día de los Muertos (Day of the Dead) mixes the Catholic All Souls Day with Mesoamerican traditions. Believers sing, pray, and make elaborate food offerings at the altars of deceased loved ones.

Roman Catholicism: A Christian religion marked by a hierarchy of priests under the pope, worship centered in a Mass, and veneration of the Virgin

African Religions in Brazil

In Brazil, the historic influence of slavery led to the creation of blended religions. Candomblé incorporates West African traditions with Catholicism. Its practices are based around a central god called Oludumaré and lesser gods called *orixas*. Candomblé followers believe that every person has a personal god who inspires and protects them. Some of these *orixas* are also Catholic saints. Rituals are performed in temples called *terreiros*, where food and animal sacrifices can be offered to the gods.

Umbanda is another Afro-Brazilian religion with multiple inspirations, including Catholic, Hindu, Buddhist, African, and indigenous traditions. Believers foster a connection to the spirit world for healing and spiritual growth.

"Candomblé" means "dance in honor of the gods." During worship, believers are guided by priests. They perform chants and trance-like dances and believe they may be temporarily possessed by orixas.

Christ the Redeemer towers over the cityscape of Rio de Janeiro in Brazil. The giant Christian monument was completed in 1931 and is positioned at the top of Mount Corcovado.

The Virgin Mary reportedly visited a peasant named Juan Diego in 1531 near Mexico City. Known as the Virgin of Guadalupe, her image is a popular symbol of Mexican faith.

Early mixtures of indigenous and Christian religions evolved out of forced conversion. Many local people adopted Catholic traditions out of necessity but then used them to disguise the indigenous traditions they weren't allowed to openly practice. Over time, distinct sets of practices blended together into new forms of **syncretic**—or combined—religions. The Aymara people in the Andes, who worship both nature-based deities and Catholic saints, provide an example of the new religious beliefs that emerged.

syncretic: Combining two distinct belief systems to create a new form.

Beyond Catholicism

Catholicism has dominated the religious landscape of Latin America for centuries. However, a recent surge of Protestant beliefs is changing the region. Evangelical and Pentecostal churches have found a unique popularity in Latin America. Currently, Protestantism is most common in poor communities. People searching for a closer connection with their religious leaders as they strive toward spiritual improvement have welcomed the change.

Although Christianity accounts for the majority of religious practices in Latin America, it coexists with a wider variety of world religions. Islam, Judaism, Hinduism, and Buddhism are also represented. Immigrants have historically transported these minority religions to Latin America.

As Africans were brought to Latin America, they were also forced to adopt Christianity. Rich traditions from West African religions persisted, however, and syncretic religions emerged from African, European, and indigenous influences. Santeria in Cuba combines Catholic and Yoruba practices, while voodoo in Haiti fuses Christianity with beliefs from Yoruba, Congo, and Taino sources.

Exuberant *dancers parade through the streets of Oruro, Bolivia, each year during Carnival. The 10-day event brings together traditional folk dances, a sacred indigenous site, and the Christian calendar.*

Evidence of the blended religious traditions in Latin America can be found in the many festivals that combine indigenous or African music, dance, and rituals with Christian holidays. Santa Semana, the week leading up to Easter, is celebrated around the region with vibrant festivities. Local patron saints are honored at certain points in the year, such as the February celebration of the Virgin de la Candelaria in Puno, Peru. In Mexico City, daily devotions are made to the Virgin of Guadalupe.

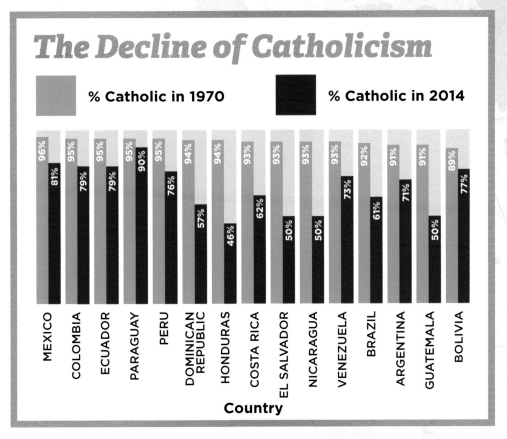

The Decline of Catholicism

■ % Catholic in 1970   ■ % Catholic in 2014

Country	% Catholic in 1970	% Catholic in 2014
MEXICO	96%	81%
COLOMBIA	95%	79%
ECUADOR	95%	79%
PARAGUAY	95%	90%
PERU	95%	76%
DOMINICAN REPUBLIC	94%	57%
HONDURAS	94%	46%
COSTA RICA	93%	62%
EL SALVADOR	93%	50%
NICARAGUA	93%	50%
VENEZUELA	93%	73%
BRAZIL	92%	61%
ARGENTINA	91%	71%
GUATEMALA	91%	50%
BOLIVIA	89%	77%

Country

Secular holidays show a pride in the ethnic identities that stayed strong through centuries of oppression. For example, residents of Tarabuco, Bolivia, remember an 1816 indigenous uprising against Spanish soldiers with the Pujllay festival. National independence celebrations also commemorate the end of colonial rule throughout the region.

3 MUSIC AND DANCE

Music and dance are hallmarks of Latin American festivals, daily life, and identity—and have been for centuries. Historical texts and **artifacts** record the role of music and dance in ancient rituals. The main instruments used by Inca, Maya, and Aztec peoples included drums, wind instruments like flutes or panpipes, and trumpets made from natural materials.

CULTURAL CONNECTIONS

Taino Arawak people in Cuba, the Dominican Republic, and Puerto Rico combined music and dance in ceremonies known as *areito*. Dancers formed rings around musicians who played drums, maracas, and scrapers.

Modern Andean folk music is made with similar instruments. Chants and instrumental Andean music can be heard throughout the highlands of Peru, Ecuador, Bolivia, and Chile. The addition of stringed instruments to traditional folk music occurred when Roman Catholic religious music mingled with indigenous rituals. Cathedrals built by Spanish and Portuguese colonists became important locations for musical performance and training. Missionaries, such as the **Jesuits**, also used music and dance to teach converts.

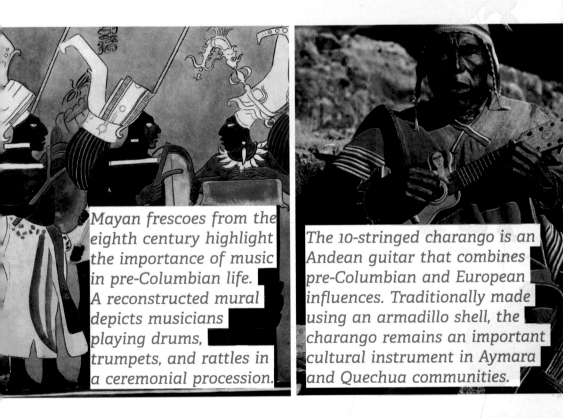

Mayan frescoes from the eighth century highlight the importance of music in pre-Columbian life. A reconstructed mural depicts musicians playing drums, trumpets, and rattles in a ceremonial procession.

The 10-stringed charango is an Andean guitar that combines pre-Columbian and European influences. Traditionally made using an armadillo shell, the charango remains an important cultural instrument in Aymara and Quechua communities.

Music and dance are deeply interconnected in the realm of Latin American popular music. Hybrid **genres** have come out of the African, European, or indigenous roots of specific regions. These include bomba, merengue, tango, and samba.

Folk Dances

Spanish and Portuguese influences can be seen in many features of traditional Latin American folk dance. Shoe-tapping, snapping, playing **castanets**, and waving scarves are all features of European dance that were adopted in colonial times. They've been incorporated into folk dances that mark special occasions and life events. Indigenous dancers commonly wear colorful, regional costumes that emphasize the movements and story of the dance. African-inspired folk dances highlight the rhythm and beat of the music with **undulating** body movements. An example of a Latin American folk dance is the Baile de la Conquista, which tells the story of the Spanish arrival in Guatemala.

Percussion is the driving musical force in the Caribbean, where bomba is popular. African slave heritage led to the emergence of bomba music in colonial Puerto Rico. Bomba rhythms are typically established with barrel drums, maracas, and two wooden sticks called *cua*.

Merengue is part of national identity in the Dominican Republic, where Merengue Day is celebrated every year on November 26. In merengue, couples dance to the sounds of accordions, drums, and saxophones.

Samba is the backbone of Brazilian music and dance. The style has deep African roots and evolved in Rio de Janeiro in the early 1900s. The genre grew in popularity and inspired new styles, such as bossa nova, a less percussive variation. Like all major Latin American music styles, samba blended diverse regional, ethnic, and historical influences to create a new art form.

Samba is a vital component of Carnival celebrations in Brazil. Extravagant parades of dancers in Rio de Janeiro and São Paulo showcase samba music, dance, and wild costumes.

Revolutionary Songs

Military **dictators** in the 19th century provoked an era of violence and social unrest in Latin America. In response, the New Song (or Nueva Canción) Movement surfaced as a tool for common people to criticize corrupt practices. The Chilean folk singer Victor Jara helped lead the movement with his social criticism through song. However, Jara was killed in 1973. Other singers, such as Mercedes Sosa of Argentina and Violeta Parra of Chile, carried on in the movement, using music to inspire others to fight for equality and social justice.

Victor Jara's musical message had lasting cultural significance. Chileans played Jara's 1971 song "The Right to Live in Peace" during demonstrations against rising metro costs in 2019.

dictator: Someone who rules a country by force.

Tango arrived on the music scene from the dance halls of Buenos Aires, Argentina. It began to develop in the 1880s from a mixture of ethnic traditions. Tango consists mainly of guitars that **serenade** partners on the dance floor. Originally marked by quick rhythms and dance steps, tango gained a slower, more **melancholy** style in the 1920s.

By the 1910s, tango was already becoming a global phenomenon. Two dancers exhibit the new ballroom style in London, England, in this photograph from 1913.

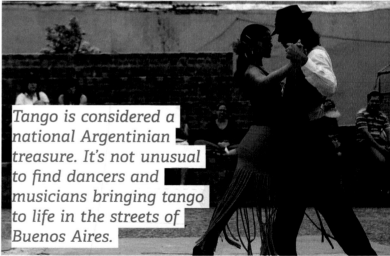

Tango is considered a national Argentinian treasure. It's not unusual to find dancers and musicians bringing tango to life in the streets of Buenos Aires.

4 LANGUAGE AND LITERATURE

Though Spanish is the dominant language across Latin America, Portuguese is the primary language spoken in Brazil. Haiti and French Guyana are the only two nations of the region in which French is widely spoken. On top of these three main tongues, many Latin Americans also speak indigenous languages. It's

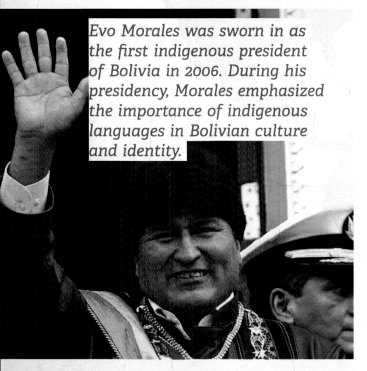

Evo Morales was sworn in as the first indigenous president of Bolivia in 2006. During his presidency, Morales emphasized the importance of indigenous languages in Bolivian culture and identity.

estimated that more than 2,000 languages were spoken in pre-Columbian Latin America, though only about 560 survive. Those languages include Nahuatl in Mexico, Quechua in the Andean region, Guarani in Paraguay, and Aymara in Peru and Bolivia.

CULTURAL CONNECTIONS

In the mid-1500s, a Spanish settler named Bartolomé de Las Casas published *A Short Account of the Destruction of the Indies*. The work called for the abolition of slavery in the Spanish colonies.

The first Latin American literary traditions predate Columbus's arrival. Because few indigenous societies had alphabetic writing systems, they used oral, or spoken, traditions for recording cultural stories and events. Mayan and Aztec peoples also made records using **pictographs**, and the Inca designed knotted ropes called quipu for recordkeeping and communication. After conquest, many of the rich oral traditions of pre-Columbian cultures

pictograph: An image-based recording of an event or story.

were captured in written form. Colonial priests and friars were part of these efforts, as were native community members who **transcribed** oral histories after learning to read and write.

Aztec codices, or books, like this were created to document life and record celebrations and events in ancient Mexico. Instead of words, the Aztecs used pictographs to record history and stories.

CULTURAL CONNECTIONS

Novelists in the 20th century celebrated African and indigenous identity by retelling traditional oral stories in modern forms. Miguel Ángel Asturias reconfigured Mayan tales in his book *Leyendas de Guatemala*, published in 1930.

In the early colonial period, Mexico and Peru became centers of creative expression. The 15th-century arrival of the printing press in Mexico encouraged literary arts. Poetry, descriptions of the conquest, and ancient regional histories created a new **canon** of Latin American literature. Sor Juana Inés de la Cruz became one of the region's first great poets in the 17th century.

Sor Juana Inés de la Cruz was born in Mexico in 1651. She became a Catholic nun so that she would have the freedom to read and compose essays, plays, and poems.

Brazilian Paolo Coelho became a best-selling author with his 1984 novel The Alchemist. The novel centers on universal themes of finding love and following your dreams.

Pablo Neruda's poetry explored Latin American identity and embraced inventive styles.

Widespread independence movements in the 19th century created new subjects and themes for Latin American novelists. Writers such as Domingo Faustino Sarmiento elevated the local landscape with rich, compelling descriptions and drew attention to injustices in modern life. Similarly, antislavery novels in Cuba became popular works that doubled as a call for social justice.

Mixing Languages

The blending of native and European languages in Latin America occurred gradually after conquest. Missionaries and indigenous people adapted native languages to the Latin alphabet. The Nahuatl language, spoken in central Mexico, was first transcribed in the Latin alphabet around 1540. Over the next century, it gradually borrowed and incorporated Spanish words. Increased cultural exchange between Spanish and indigenous groups led to languages with overlapping words and structures. The exchange went both ways, and indigenous words have also been integrated into Latin American Spanish.

In 1945, Gabriela Mistral from Chile became the first Latin American poet to receive the Nobel Prize in Literature. Pablo Neruda from

Magic Realism

In the 20th century, Latin American novelists developed distinctive literary styles that earned international attention. Writers such as Argentine Jorge Luis Borges challenged the norms of fiction writing and laid the groundwork for a genre called **magic realism**. This style blends ordinary and fantastical elements within a story. Magic realism is often linked with the Guatemalan writer Miguel Ángel Asturias and his 1946 book *El Señor Presidente*. The style was also developed in *One Hundred Years of Solitude* by Colombian writer Gabriel García Márquez, and *The House of the Spirits* by Chilean author Isabel Allende.

Chile also earned the honor in 1971. In today's literary culture, Edwidge Danticat from Haiti, Paulo Coehlo from Brazil, Junot Díaz from the Dominican Republic, and many others have brought Latin American storytelling to the world stage.

COUNTRY	INDIGENOUS POPULATION	NUMBER OF INDIGENOUS LANGUAGES
Mexico	16.83 million	67
Peru	7.60 million	47
Guatemala	5.88 million	24
Bolivia	4.12 million	33
Colombia	1.53 million	65

magic realism: A literary style that combines fantastical and ordinary elements.

5 VISUAL ARTS

A wide variety of pre-Columbian art, artifacts, and architecture have been preserved as part of Latin American history. The range of styles, materials, and subjects has shed light on the unique cultures of the period, while their similarities point to the historic exchange of goods and ideas that must have occurred. After European conquest introduced new technologies to the region, the movement of people and goods across ancient tribal or national boundaries became easier. As a result, colonial artistic styles spread throughout Latin America. For the next 300 years, Latin American art was mainly influenced by the trends and styles of Europe.

Independence movements in the 1800s inspired new artistic subjects and techniques, and regional styles took root. Within these new styles, artists began to more openly embrace African and indigenous influences. This allowed them to highlight the mixtures of history and culture that made their region unique. At the same time, **tensions** between European and indigenous or African identities became more distinct.

Diego Rivera's murals in the Zócalo, the main square in the heart of Mexico City, express the complexities of Mexican history in a fluid, detailed, and artistic form.

tension: A strained political or social relationship.

The Mexican **mural** movement in the early 1900s placed these social and racial tensions in the spotlight. Diego Rivera, José Clemente Orozco, and David Alfaro Siqueiros painted public walls in Mexico in the 1930s and 1940s with fresh interpretations of Mexican life and Mexican people. Rivera's murals in Mexico City traced the nation's history and emphasized the injustices that were especially damaging to indigenous communities and working-class people. At the same time, he highlighted the strength and beauty of indigenous culture.

CULTURAL CONNECTIONS

The architectural innovations of Oscar Niemeyer, a Brazilian, earned global acclaim. His design for the Niterói Museum of Contemporary Art in Rio de Janeiro is a striking feat of engineering and artistry.

Frida Kahlo was another 20th-century artist who presented a new perspective of Mexican life. Her engaging and intimate

mural: A painting on a ceiling or wall, often in a public place.

self-portraits explored themes of suffering, female identity, relationships, and Mexican heritage. Today, Kahlo is one of the best-known Latin American artists around the world.

Compared with the monumental works of the Mexican muralists, Kahlo's self-portraits are quite small and contained. Nonetheless, they manage to appeal to large and diverse groups of people.

The artists Frida Kahlo and Diego Rivera, seen here, married each other in 1929. Kahlo's painting The Two Fridas can be seen on the studio wall alongside other works.

Arpilleras

A folk art form became a powerful tool for social commentary in the 1970s and 1980s. During this time, Chile was under the tyrannical, or all-powerful, rule of dictator Augusto Pinochet. The period was characterized by governmental oppression. People throughout the nation were routinely arrested, tortured, killed, or "disappeared" for speaking against the government. In response to this crisis, women in Chile began crafting *arpilleras* to record their struggles. *Arpilleras* are three-dimensional patchwork tapestries that create a scene or story. In a time of danger and fear, *arpilleras* provided a creative outlet for Chilean women to express themselves and document their lives.

Many indigenous people and families earn a living by creating traditional folk art and handcrafts.

Arpilleras *were originally made to record oppression in Chile, but the art form has spread to other Latin American countries as well.*

Echoes of Maya and Aztec codices can be seen in the grid-like format and simplified symbols chosen by Joaquín Torres-García.

Another uniquely Latin American artistic movement is Universal Constructivism, introduced by the Uruguayan artist Joaquín Torres-García in the 1930s. The style drew on Aztec, Incan, African, and other art styles to find common symbols. It also distanced itself from European artistic traditions, relying instead on earth tones and

CULTURAL CONNECTIONS

Latin American handicrafts represent a link to indigenous cultural identity. Creating pottery, woven **textiles**, embroidery, wood carvings, ceremonial masks, and other forms of folk art helps preserve artistic and cultural traditions.

geometric figures that were more closely associated with pre-Columbian art. Although Torres-García pursued art that was free from European influences, most Latin American art has developed out of the combination of local and global styles.

Latin American Cinema

Beginning in the 1930s, film became an important medium for Latin American artists who had global aspirations. In 1960, a Mexican film titled *Macario* became the first Oscar-nominated Latin American film. In 1985, *The Official Story* from Argentina was the first Latin American film to win an Oscar. Latin American filmmakers in recent decades have received praise for both foreign-language and English-language films at the Academy Awards. Guillermo del Toro, Alejandro González Iñárritu, and Alfonso Cuarón are all Oscar-winning Mexican directors. Their success highlights the spread of artistic ideas from Latin America to the world.

6 POPULAR CULTURE

Latin American **popular culture** has been widely adopted all across the globe. Whether it's taken the form of energy-filled sporting events, gripping **telenovelas**, glamorous runway fashions, or the latest musical hits, Latin Americans in every field have attracted the world's attention.

Food in Latin America

Latin America has contributed a number of staple foods to the global market over time. After Europeans' first landfall in the Americas, they began trading for and with local foods. These included corn, avocados, tomatoes, pumpkins, papayas, and chocolate from Mexico, cacao from Venezuela, the tea-like drink yerba maté from Paraguay, pineapples from Brazil, strawberries from Chile, potatoes from the Andes, and peanuts from throughout South America. These crops, now part of a common global diet, have had a great influence on what and how people eat. They've also been featured in regional Latin American dishes, which are as numerous and diverse as the people who make them.

popular culture: Cultural products such as music, art, fashion, television, and radio that are consumed by many people in a society.

Soccer is the most popular sport in Latin America, and fans around the world cheer on their national teams. The

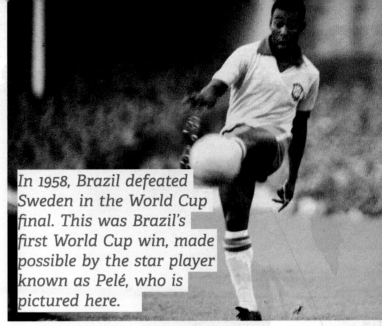

In 1958, Brazil defeated Sweden in the World Cup final. This was Brazil's first World Cup win, made possible by the star player known as Pelé, who is pictured here.

game is called *fútbol* in Spanish or *futebol* in Portuguese, and it arrived in South America in the late 1800s. Introduced in Buenos Aires, Argentina, by British immigrants and European sailors, soccer quickly caught on across the region. The sport requires minimal setup, equipment, and space, making it an easy game to play in any community. Soccer is the most popular sport in the world, and Latin Americans are famously loyal to their local teams and clubs. Many Latin American teams have been launched to global fame as well. Brazil is a five-time Men's World Cup winner, while Argentina has secured the coveted trophy twice.

Television provides access to two important sources of Latin American entertainment: sporting events—mainly soccer—and telenovelas. Trendy throughout the region, telenovelas are aired on daytime and nighttime television. They capture viewers' attention with relatable dramas rooted in family themes and romance. Telenovelas evolved

The American sitcom Ugly Betty was based on a Colombian telenovela titled Yo Soy Betty, La Fea. The show tracked the misadventures of a brilliant but awkward heroine.

from popular stories in **graphic novels** and radio programs. They found a new and effective format with the spread of television in the mid-1900s. More than a half-century later, dozens of telenovelas air every day. They are broadcast in several seasons that last until the main characters find a solution to their problems, commonly in the form of a happy ending or wedding. Watching telenovelas is a popular family activity, and the latest plot twists make for good discussion in community gatherings.

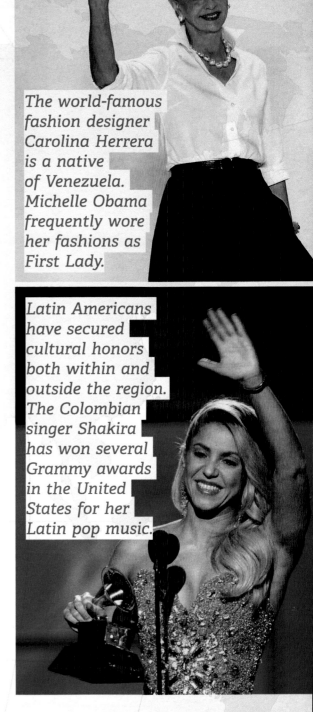

The world-famous fashion designer Carolina Herrera is a native of Venezuela. Michelle Obama frequently wore her fashions as First Lady.

Latin Americans have secured cultural honors both within and outside the region. The Colombian singer Shakira has won several Grammy awards in the United States for her Latin pop music.

graphic novel: A story told in a comic-book style.

The Olympics in Latin America

The Olympics have been held in Latin American countries on two occasions, both marked by controversy. The 1968 Summer Olympics were held in Mexico during a difficult social and political period. The games began just weeks after a government-perpetrated attack against Mexican students protesting for social and education reform. The attack became known as the Tlatelolco massacre. Several decades later, the 2016 Summer Olympics were planned in Rio de Janiero, Brazil. This event heightened existing tensions in the host country. Costly preparations for the Olympics highlighted the severe gap between wealthy and poor Brazilians and spotlighted many unresolved political issues.

More than 11 million Brazilians live in shantytowns called favelas. Most favelas lack access to clean water and proper sanitation.

Modern popular culture in Latin America is wildly diverse, just like the landscapes, climates, and people who've developed it over the centuries. It's constantly changing and growing, incorporating new influences while also preserving important traditions. These forces will undoubtedly continue to define and shape collective and local Latin American identity for years to come.

Baseball is a classic sport for children and adults in the Dominican Republic. Skilled players from the nation are frequently recruited to play for professional U.S. teams.

GLOSSARY

artifact: Something made by humans in the past.

canon: A body of important works.

castanet: Rhythm instrument made of two hard shells that are held in the hand and clicked together.

exuberant: Joyfully enthusiastic.

genre: A type or style of music, dance, or another art form.

hierarchy: A system that places people in a series of levels with varying importance or status.

immigrant: One who comes to a country to settle there.

melancholy: Sad and subdued.

nomadic: Having to do with people who move from place to place.

secular: Not religious.

serenade: To sing or play romantic music for someone.

solstice: The time of year when the sun is farthest north (the summer solstice, about June 21), or farthest south (the winter solstice, about December 21) of the equator.

transcribe: To make a written copy.

undulating: Rising and falling, or moving in a waving fashion.

FOR MORE INFORMATION

BOOKS:

Nichols, Susan. *The People and Culture of Latin America*. New York, NY: Rosen Publishing, 2018.

Orgullo, Marisa. *Celebrating Hispanic Heritage Month!* New York, NY: PowerKids Press, 2019.

Tyler, Madeline. *Cultural Contributions from Latin America: Tortillas, Color TV, and More*. New York, NY: PowerKids Press, 2019.

WEBSITES:

Aztecs, Maya, and Inca for Kids
www.ducksters.com/history/aztec_maya_inca.php
Information about the three main civilizations of ancient Mesoamerica and South America are presented on this site.

Latin American Art and Architecture
www.scholastic.com/browse/article.jsp?id=3753884
This website provides an in-depth description of major movements in Latin American art.

National Geographic Kids: Brazil
kids.nationalgeographic.com/explore/countries/brazil/
This website provides an overview of the people, landscape, and history of Brazil, which is the largest country in Latin America.

INDEX